CULTIVATE YOUR

content

Create Strategic Content That Attracts Your Dream Clients Using Human Design

A companion workbook to the book, *Cultivate You!*

Lise Cartwright | HustleandGroove.com

Hello Creative Business Owner

Are you ready to create a consistent income business based on what FEELS easy and fun for you?

With this workbook you will be able to create an action plan to that brings you consistent income month after month. No more feast or famine cycles for you!

You've made a great decision, here's why...

✓ Creating an online business that harnesses your strengths allows you to focus on the tactics and strategies that feel easy and fun for you. It allows you to connect with your audience in a way that comes **natural** to you. This leads to easy cash flow and no one-size-fits-all strategies in sight!

✓ When you combine your you-nique gifts, strengths, and talents to craft your messages, you're able to step into truly authentic content and offers that resonates with your people. You don't need to use fancy words or fancy tactics to attract your ideal customer. Be you. Show that you genuinely care. Empower and inspire your audience by sharing the authentic, raw you. Since you're here to truly make a difference in the lives of your people, they are much more likely to want to buy more from—and work with—someone they feel they **connect** with.

✓ On top of being easy and fun, when you focus on you doing you in your business, you're able to **sell** to your audience will ease. By leaning into being more you, you stand out in your space because you're creating offers that provide value and changes lives. Marketing your business doesn't mean you need to sell your soul. Instead, when you do what comes naturally to you, cash flows freely.

Contents
it's time to discover what's inside!

Congratulations on purchasing this **Workbook!** If you haven't purchased the first book in this series, *Cultivate You!*, please do that here to get the best experience: www.hustleandgroove.com/cybbook

Do what feels right to you, not what someone else tells you works. Listen to what lights you up and create from that space...

LISE CARTWRIGHT, BEST SELLING AUTHOR AND CREATIVE BUSINESS COACH

Introduction

you do you!

I can hardly believe this is the final book in the Cultivate Your Business series.

What started out as one book quickly turned into five micro-books.

And I think (but shhhh, don't tell the other books) that this book is my favorite.

More specifically, the content I'm going to be sharing with you inside these pages.

This whole book is going to change the way you approach content creation. Particularly if, like I was, you're under the misconception that the more content you create, the faster your audience will find you.

Only it doesn't quite work that way, does it?

And it's not your fault that you believe this.

The phrase *"Content is King/Queen"* has led many online business owners to produce content after content without any real strategy to it. And therein lies the rub.

The gurus go on and on about how *"Content is King/Queen"* but they don't back any of that up with real direction.

Because... well, then you wouldn't buy their stuff!

So how should we approach content creation instead?

I'm so glad you asked!

Introduction
you do you!

Rather than feeling like you have to write a blog post a week, or create three YouTube videos a week, it's about creating strategic content based on the offers you have.

I call this Discoverable Content.

It's about being discoverable versus visible.

What's the difference?

Discoverable is when people find you based on what they are searching for.

Visibility is showing up in someone's social media feeds without any prompts from them.

There's a time and place for both.

But inside the pages of this book, we're going to lean heavily towards discoverability.

But first, let's start with a story.

Back in 2012, after I quit my full-time job to become a full-time freelance writer, I kept hearing that phrase... "Content is King!"

And I took it to heart.

It made so much sense to me at the time.

After all, I was a freelance writer; of course, I needed to produce a lot of content.

Introduction
you do you!

So I started writing two blog posts a week.

It would take me about four hours per blog post.

And these weren't short posts. I'm a prolific writer and I tend to have a lot to say, so each of these posts would be anywhere between 1,500 to 3,000 words.

I also had four ongoing freelance writing clients too.

My life became all about content.

But that content I was writing for my blogs... it wasn't meaningful. It didn't really showcase my personality.

If we're being honest (and we are), a lot of this content was regurgitated. I would simply see what others were doing and rewrite the content based on my experiences.

And while that's not a bad way to create content, it's not content that connects with your audience.

It's not content that your audience will remember you for.

In fact, what will often happen is that your audience will read this type of content and nod their head and think something along the lines of, *"Oh yeah, I already knew this..."*

Instead of, *"OMG, how on earth did I not know this already?!"*

Introduction
you do you!

The latter is what happens when you start writing strategic, discoverable content using your authentic voice.

I didn't figure this out until 2019. Seven years after I'd been running my business.

Oof, that's painful to write.

It also explains the 400+ blog posts that live on my website, with at least 70% of those falling into the regurgitated content pile.

But it's not all doom and gloom. In 2020, when I discovered Human Design and really found my authentic voice and magnetic messaging, that all changed.

And so did the belief that I needed to be creating content on a regular basis.

At the time of writing this book (July 2024), I haven't written a blog post in over seven months. Yet the traffic to my blog posts has increased.

And no, I'm not running any paid ad campaigns.

It's all through the power of Discoverable Content. Which also leads to automated sales...

But I won't spoil the fun!

You'll learn all this and more as you work your way through this book. So all that's left to do is get your pen handy (or your keyboard) because it's time to get to work!

CHAPTER ONE

it all starts with messaging...

ideas...

ideas...

In this chapter, I want to walk you through what I like to call magnetic messaging. And it's not just the messaging that you're putting out on social media, although that's a layer of it.

This is about nailing the things that you say again and again.

Think about this type of messaging as content that you could put on your homepage, your about me page, or what you might share on your social profiles.

Some might consider it part of their brand messaging, and if that helps you understand this point faster, let's say that it is (but it's so much more than that).

As you work your way through this book, I want you to filter <u>everything</u> through your Human Design type, strategy, authority, and profile numbers.

I want to make sure that you don't skip this because ultimately, when it comes to running an aligned business, the way that happens is by ensuring that we follow our strategy and authority, and then our profile numbers layer over the top.

This is what makes you, *you*.

But often, our profile numbers can also be where we get conditioning coming in. So it's important to be aware of this as you work on and in your business.

Let's get back to what we're here to talk about: magnetic messaging.

This is about being clear on the things that you believe. It comes back to your core values.

And this is not just in business. This is part of your life.

On a business level, it is about knowing and living what your core values are.

What are the things that you believe when it comes to what you do?

What are the things that you are trying to help your overarching audience achieve?

We can summarize this down to:

- What you believe in
- What you stand for
- Being consistent in what you say *everywhere*

So that when your audience starts to hear you and see these words, they start to associate them with you.

Here are some examples of what I say to get your own juices flowing:

I'm sure that if you've been in my world for a little bit; if you've come to any of my workshops or trainings, you would have heard me say: *"It does get to be easy and fun."*

Or *"If it's not easy and fun, why do it?"*

"It should be easy, fun, and profitable."

"There are no one-size-fits-all strategies when it comes to running your business."

"You get to do you in your business."

"Just because you can, doesn't mean you should."

This is my magnetic messaging. This is the core brand messaging that I'm talking about here. This is weaved into everything that I do.

This is the core of how I create my offers. What I put out into the world starts with this messaging. These phrases are like little prompts that keep me focused on how I help my audience.

This is what I want you to start to think about, particularly as you start creating your offers and building out your content.

This is that foundational piece.

To help you figure this out, work through the following exercises.

Question One:
What are three words that describe the personality of your brand (e.g., vibrant, professional, compassionate)?

Exercise: Write a short story or a blog post from the perspective of your brand. Use the three words you chose to infuse the narrative with your brand's personality.

Question Two:
What are the top five values that are most important to your brand?

Exercise: For each value, list a real example of how your business embodies this value in its operations, products, or services.

Question Three:

Who is your ideal customer? Create a detailed persona including their age, interests, challenges, and desires.

AI Prompt: Hi there. I need your help. I want you to act as if you were a marketing coach for solopreneurs. I would like you to create a detailed persona for my ideal customer [who they are] and include their age, interests, challenges, and desires.

Exercise: Write a direct message to this persona explaining why your brand's perspective is uniquely suited to help them.

Question Four:

Why did you start your business? Beyond making money, what motivates you every day?

Exercise: Describe a moment when you felt truly impactful through your work—how did it make you feel and how did it align with your business mission?

Question Five:

What are the key messages you want your clients or customers to remember about your brand?

Exercise: Create a slogan or a tagline that encapsulates your key messages in a concise and catchy way.

Question Six:

What change or transformation do you offer your customers? How are they different after interacting with your brand?

Exercise: Develop a before and after scenario to visibly illustrate the transformation customers experience. *(Refer to one of your Tangible Offer Framework documents—which you'll find inside the book, Cultivate Your Offers— and pull together Island A and Island B—create a story around this.)*

Question Seven:

What common objections or hesitations might your customers have about your brand or products?

Exercise: Write a FAQ section addressing these concerns directly, using persuasive but understanding language.

Question Eight:

How will your core messaging influence your offers, content creation, and overall marketing strategy?

Exercise: Map out how your core messages align with different aspects of your marketing, such as social media posts, email campaigns, and product offerings.

Take your time working through these questions and exercises.

This is important, foundational work that informs a lot of your positioning moving forward.

In the next chapter, we're going to start using this messaging. So make sure you're ready to dive in.

Notes
capture your ideas

Notes
capture your ideas

Notes

capture your ideas

CHAPTER TWO

your offers and

audience...

ideas...

ideas...

Now that you've got your magnetic messaging nailed down, let's review the offers you have and the audience for each of your offers.

The goal is to have an aligned offer suite that reflects your magnetic messaging.

Type-based prompts to keep you aligned:

MANIFESTORS: What do you feel compelled to create? Make sure you inform anyone around you when you decide to move forward.

GENERATORS: What are you noticing? What patterns do you see? What questions are you being asked? Remember, you need to create in response to external stimuli.

MANIFESTING GENERATORS: What do you notice in your business? What do your analytics tell you? What questions are you being asked or noticing? Remember, you need to create in response to external stimuli.

PROJECTORS: What is the best way for you to share your zone of genius? What would you create without attachment to the outcome? Your strategy is to wait for the invitation. What have you been invited to recently?

REFLECTORS: What have you experienced in the last 30 days that you continue to be excited and energized about? Remember, you don't make decisions quickly. Experience things, feel things, and ultimately, do what feels good to you.

Before you do anything, make sure that you have a copy of the *Cultivate Your Offers workbook* because that is where we do a deep dive into the Tangible Offer Framework, a core process for ensuring that the offers you create are aligned.

Your Human Design strategy determines how you're designed to interact with the world. In your business, this means how you're designed to create your offers.

Keep it simple and ensure that whenever you're creating an offer, you're solving a problem that your audience wants solved (or believes that if they could just solve this one thing, it would make a world of difference).

But how does this help you cultivate your content?

I'm glad you asked!

It all starts with the Tangible Offer Framework. Inside that framework, there are eight questions designed to:

- Determine the audience for the offer (you'll complete a TO document for every offer you create),
- Determine the transformation you're looking to help them achieve.

It also helps you figure out what you'll include in the offer, the type of offer it could be, bonuses, etc.

The point being... we NEVER create content just for the sake of creating content.

So where does that leave us then?

Instead, we're focused on creating strategic, discoverable content.

And your content creation starts with you having a clear picture of:

- The audience for each offer
- The problem you're solving with the offer
- What your audience wants their life to look like after their problem has been solved

I'm certain that you already have some offers created, so let's ensure that your magnetic messaging is also reflected in those offers.

Work through the following questions:

Question One:

Review your offer suite. For each offer, ask yourself the question: *Can I easily say which of my core messages is reflected in this offer?*

Question Two:

If you have sales pages created, review these for each offer and ask yourself: *Is my magnetic messaging reflected in the words and images on this page?*

If you answer "no" to either of these questions, take the time to make the necessary tweaks and adjustments.

Then come and join us in the next section, where we'll start creating content!

Notes
capture your ideas

Notes
capture your ideas

CHAPTER THREE

create content that attracts dream clients

ideas...

ideas...

I'm so excited for this section!

I want to introduce you to the Discoverable Content System. This system is what allows you to create strategic content that attracts your dream clients.

Discoverable Content meets your audience where they are and when they are looking for a solution.

It is the complete opposite of chasing your clients or searching for customers. Discoverable Content is the best organic and free way to bring people into your world and build know, like, and trust factors.

There are two types of Discoverable Content:

Macro Content:

This is long-form content. It's what marketers might refer to as 'top of funnel' content or TOFU (not the edible kind!). It's content that has the highest chance of showing up in search engines based on what your audience is searching for.

Micro Content:

This is short-form content. It's shared on social media platforms and is created through repurposing. It's typically a smaller sub-category of your main content.

Discoverable Content provides you with a way to sell your offers right when your ideal customer is looking for a solution to their problem.

The goal is to create macro content first, then micro content (if you wish). This is ALWAYS about following your energy, strategy, and authority.

To be clear: YOU DO NOT HAVE TO BE ON SOCIAL MEDIA CONSTANTLY TO MAKE MONEY! But you do have to be showing up for your audience in your own authentic way.

The first step in this process is to fill out a Messaging Organizer for each offer.

Step 1: Complete Your Messaging Organizer

Follow the questions below to complete this for yourself:

Question One: Island A / Challenges. Lay of the land through their eyes. What are 8-10 challenges that your audience has right now? You can either think of this in relation to your book(s) and/or your offers. Ideally, these are written as if your ideal customer was talking to you. So use the word "I" when writing this down.

Question Two: Island B. What does life look like for them once challenges are solved? What are 8-10 things they want to be able to do right now if they didn't have the problem/challenge? This should be focused on what you decided on in Island A. In other words, your solution statements should solve each problem identified above. Again, use the word "I" and "I'm" when writing this, as if your ideal customer was chatting with you.

Question Three: What myths/beliefs/fears does my audience have around this offer? In other words, what do you need your ideal customer to know to make an informed decision? What are they worried about? Why don't they believe they can do this? What beliefs do they have that are incorrect? What guru have they followed that led them astray? This content is what you'll be using on your sales page, in your sales emails, and in any micro content.

Once you've got the answers to these three questions, you're going to complete the following exercises (this will all be through your own lens, aka your perspective).

Exercise One: What's your perspective on Island A? Paste the Island A list, then add "BECAUSE..." after each point.

Exercise Two: What's your perspective on Island B? Paste the Island B list, then add "HOW TO GO ABOUT..." before each point.

Exercise Three: Paste the myths/beliefs/fears list, then decide HOW you'll address each of these. Consider case studies, previous results from people you've worked with, testimonials, examples, stories, etc.

Step 2: Choose a Content Platform

The next step in this process is to decide on your ONE macro (long-form) content platform.

The most common options are:

- A blog
- A podcast
- A YouTube channel
- A book (this takes the longest to implement, so I don't recommend it initially)

These can all be repurposed into all three options, but I recommend focusing on ONE platform first. Once you have a Virtual Assistant (VA), you can start to repurpose into all of these platforms if you wish.

DECISION: *Which long-form content platform will you focus on?*

Step 3: Create Your Content

The next step is to create, publish, and optimize your content!

Ideally, you will want to have at least 1-3 pieces of Discoverable Content (macro) published for each offer.

To create your Discoverable Content, review your messaging organizer and use the section where you look at things from your perspective.

Use any of the notes you made as prompts to generate content from.

You might also find it helpful to use tools like **AnswerThePublic** to understand what your audience is searching for around your offer topic or transformation.

The long-term goal is to create all of the content (identified inside your messaging organizer) for your offers over the next 6-12 months, then repurpose into micro content if you wish.

Step 4: Share Your Content

Now that you have some Discoverable Content created, you'll want to share it.

Start by scheduling it to share on your social media profiles. Then, add a link inside your social media bios to your long-form content.

If you have an email list, I'd recommend sharing your content inside your weekly emails, as part of your welcome sequence, and in any other sequences where it makes sense to do so.

And finally, when you're ready, consider putting a paid traffic campaign in place for your Discoverable Content.

RESOURCES: Messaging Organizer and Discoverable Content Planner (available inside the Resources Hub).

Now that you've got your initial Discoverable Content pieces created, let's dive into how you can use Human Design to amplify this content.

Notes
capture your ideas

Notes
capture your ideas

Notes
capture your ideas

CHAPTER FOUR

using human design
to craft content that
connects & converts

ideas...

ideas...

This is something that I have wanted to do for a while, and I'm super excited that you're getting access to it right here inside this book.

When it comes to creating content using Human Design, we can do this by using the HD chart.

You don't need to know your audience's chart to be able to apply what I'm going to share with you here.

You just need to understand the key elements that will help you craft content that connects with your audience and then optimize it so that it also converts them into subscribers and buyers.

Once your initial Discoverable Content pieces are created, you can do one of two things:

1. Go back through your long-form Discoverable Content and apply what you'll learn here, or
2. Create new content that is more focused on the elements we're going to cover below.

It's your choice!

This section is going to be split into eight exercises, and all of these exercises are designed to help you come up with content based on the Human Design chart.

So it helps if you have a really good understanding of each center and the individual gates.

You can use this free tool to help you out: www.humandesign.tools.

It will allow you to get an overview and deep dive.

Ready? Let's dive into the exercises!

Exercise 1: Identifying Your Audience's Pain Points

Step 1: Write down the main pain point or challenge your audience faces that your offer aims to solve (you'll want to do this for each offer you have). This will form the foundation of your sales content.

Step 2: How does your offer alleviate this pain point? Write down the unique solution your offer provides.

Exercise 2: Identifying Your Human Design Type, Strategy, and Authority

Step 3: Write down your Human Design type, strategy, and authority in your own words.

Step 4: Reflect on your understanding of these. How do these characteristics affect the way you perceive and communicate ideas to your audience?

Exercise 3: Understanding Your Throat Center

Step 5: Look at your Human Design chart. What gates/channels in your throat center are active? Circle them below.

GATE 23

This is the gate of assimilation. The voice of this gate is either: *I know or not.*

GATE 62

This is the gate of details. The voice of this gate is either: *I think or not.*

GATE 56

This is the gate of the storyteller. The voice of this gate is either: *I believe or not.*

GATE 16

This is the gate of enthusiasm. The voice of this gate is either: *I experiment (I identify) or not.*

GATE 20

This is the gate of in the now. The voice of this gate is either: *I am now or not.*

GATE 31

This is the gate of influence. The voice of this gate is either: *I lead or not.*

GATE 35

This is the gate of change. The voice of this gate is either: *I experience (I feel) or not.*

GATE 12

This is the gate of caution. The voice of this gate is either: *I know I can try or not.*

GATE 45

This is the gate of the King or Queen. The voice of this gate is either: *I have or not.*

GATE 33

This is the gate of retreat or privacy. The voice of this gate is either: *I remember or not.*

GATE 8

This is the gate of contribution. The voice of this gate is either: *I know I can make a contribution or not.*

Step 6: Based on the gates you have active, how can you use these insights in your communication and content creation? In other words... what's the easiest way for you to communicate?

🎤 **Don't have any active gates in your Throat Center?** *This means you have complete flexibility in the way that you communicate and explain things. Follow your strategy and authority to guide you on what feels right for you. It also means that you're a voice for others. Focus on creating content that highlights your audience's hidden fears/pains/challenges. The things they might not want to share.*

Exercise 4: Assessing Your Audience's Head Center

Step 7: Consider a scenario where your audience has an undefined or open head center. Based on this, list potential doubts, questions, or worries they may have as it pertains to your offer.

Remember: This is a pressure center. If this is open/undefined for your audience, they may suffer from worrying about things that don't matter and feel pressured to answer all the questions.

Step 8: How can your content address these concerns? Write down ideas for blog posts, social media updates, and email content that would answer these questions or alleviate these doubts. This is all through the lens of your offer.

Exercise 5: Analyzing Your Audience's Root Center

Step 9: Similarly, consider a scenario where your audience has an undefined or open root center. What pressures might they be feeling? List potential stressors or sources of rushing, hurrying through things to relieve the pressure.

Step 10: Generate content ideas that can help your audience handle these pressures through the lens of your offer. Consider advice, tips, or insights you can provide to help them manage stress and avoid rushing decisions.

Exercise 6: Evaluating Your Audience's Spleen Center

Step 11: If your audience has an undefined or open spleen center, they might harbor certain fears or concerns. They may experience holding on to things that aren't good for them for fear of letting go. What might these fears be in relation to your offer?

Step 12: Based on the fears you've identified, generate content ideas that can help your audience address these fears. This might include reassurances, strategies for overcoming fear, or success stories from clients who have overcome similar fears, particularly important for your sales content.

Exercise 7: Aligning Your Content With Your Offer

Step 13: Write down the main result or transformation you're offering to your audience with this offer. What problem are you solving for them?

Step 14: Now, go back to the insights you gathered from the three centers—the head, root, and spleen centers. Based on your understanding of what your audience might be experiencing, and using your strategy and authority, how can you create content that helps allay these fears and worries while promoting your offer?

> **Remember**: The goal here is to use your understanding of your audience and your own unique communication style, as determined by your Human Design, to create content that resonates and persuades. The more deeply you understand both, the more effective your content will be.

Exercise 8: General Content Creation by Human Design Type

Now, based on your Human Design type, decide on the approach you will take to create your content:

- **Manifestors**: What unique perspective do you bring to your audience based on your offer? What type of content will you create? Use your authority to determine the angle of your content.
- **Generators**: Use your gut instinct to respond to the ideas you have gathered. How would you approach these issues or questions? Write down your insights.
- **Manifesting Generators**: What triggers your sacral? Is there a faster or more efficient way to address these topics? Write down your innovative ideas.
- **Projectors**: Use your authority to guide your content creation. Share your insights and wisdom based on what you know. Write about your unique discoveries, the things you weren't invited to share but are bursting to tell someone about!
- **Reflectors**: Follow your energy. What topics are you excited or passionate about? Generate content based on these interests. Content batching works well for you.

Understanding your audience's needs and your unique approach to addressing these needs can greatly improve the effectiveness of your content, particularly when you focus on creating content around your offers.

Remember: *This is all about using your Human Design type, strategy, and authority to guide you to the content you create, but to also do it through the lens of your offer and your audience and what they are struggling with.*

You could go down the entire route of using every single center in the Human Design chart and writing content that addresses the open, undefined, or not-self themes of them.

The open head, defined root, open spleen, open throat, and open heart centers (and their gates) are where I recommend you focus your content if you're doing business-to-business.

If your business is in the business-to-consumer bucket, then I'd create content based on the open head, open root, open heart, open G, and open throat centers (and their gates).

I'm certain that you're going to experience a lot of "AHA" moments as you go through the exercises and discover how easy it becomes to create content when you start implementing Human Design into your content creation process.

Let's dive into the final chapter where we'll talk about optimizing your content and profiles in more detail.

Notes

capture your ideas

Notes
capture your ideas

CHAPTER FIVE

optimizing content to sell on autopilot

ideas...

ideas...

Now that you've got all this beautiful content created, what to do next? I'm glad you asked, my little grasshopper...

Let's start with your main, long-form content.

Optimizing Your Long-form Content

Follow these steps:

Step 1: Add a main image for your content (header image for a blog post, podcast cover graphic, YouTube thumbnail, etc).

Depending on the type of platform, you might include words on the image. For example, if you're creating a thumbnail image for your YouTube channel, then you'll want to have a clear title that attracts your ideal customer.

Here's an example from a video I created that talks about the Discoverable Content system:

You can check out the live video here: https://www.youtube.com/watch?v=oP55oJKxIqk

Step 2: Choose one main keyword (which is typically a phrase based on what your audience is searching for in relation to your offer) and then 3-5 long-tail keywords that are similar.

I recommend using tools like AnswerThePublic to get a good idea of what these might be, but also using your favorite AI tool can help you with this.

AI Prompt: *Hey there. You're now a marketing coach who specializes in helping online business owners optimize their content through smart search engine optimization strategies. I'm writing a [blog post/podcast episode/video] about [your topic]. The main CTA for this piece of content is to direct my ideal customer to this offer [your offer]. Can you help me identify a main keyword that I'll use in the title, meta description, and throughout the content, as well as 3-5 similar keywords I can also use?*

Step 3: Optimize your content with metadata using Yoast (if on WordPress) and TubeBuddy (YouTube). These two tools will help you do most of the heavy SEO lifting.

Or you can do this manually by ensuring that you have:

- Your keyword in the title
- Your keyword in the description/first line of content
- Your keyword in at least one heading
- Your keyword mentioned in at least 5% of the content
- Any images have an alt tag with the keyword in it (and the title of the image also)

Include a clear call-to-action—either to a freebie or to your offer.

PRO TIP: I'd recommend the call-to-action always be to your offer, but sometimes your focus might be on list building.

Step 4: Include hyperlinks to other content and external resources. 2-3 times in blog posts, once in a video, once in a podcast episode, etc.

Once your long-form content is optimized, we can turn our attention to other areas where your audience will be engaging with your content.

Optimizing Your Emails

An area where I see a lot of people miss out on sales is inside their emails.

I'm a huge fan of building an online community on a platform that I own. For me, that happens in two areas:

- My private membership and course area
- My email list

Let's focus on the latter.

So how do you optimize your emails to sell for you on autopilot?

It's simple. We implement the 'soft sell PS strategy.'

It's been called many things, but I call it this because it's focused on each Human Design strategy.

Below are each type and some wording you might use in the PS of an email...

MANIFESTORS: Your strategy is to INFORM. Unapologetically sharing what you feel the urge to create and move forward with.

In your SELLING activities, when presenting the opportunity for people to buy from you, this looks like ensuring that when you're informing, whether that's via email, social media, or whatever medium you're using to connect with your audience, you're providing a link to your offer(s) as well, at the end of your content.

PS Example:
"I'm bursting at the seams to get this into your hands. If you're onboard with what I've said, come and check out xxx".

GENERATORS: Your strategy is to RESPOND. To respond to external ideas, to the things that the Universe puts in front of you.

In your SELLING activities, when presenting the opportunity for people to buy from you, this looks like ensuring that you provide your audience with the opportunity to RESPOND to your ideas.

Provide your audience with options to choose from when you're sharing content with them in response to the offers you've created.

PS Example:
"If this resonated with you, here are [x number] ways I can support you right now:
- *Xxx offer*
- *Abc offer*
- *123 offers"*
-

MANIFESTING GENERATORS: Your strategy is to RESPOND and INFORM.

In your SELLING activities, when presenting the opportunity for people to buy from you, this looks like ensuring that when you're informing (after responding), whether that's via email, social media, or whatever medium you're using to connect with your audience, you're providing a link to your offer(s).

PS Example:
"If this resonated with you and if you're excited by what I've said, here's how you can dive deeper xxx".

PROJECTORS: Your strategy is to be INVITED. This means that before you give advice, you've got to wait for the person to ask for it.

In your SELLING activities, your approach is a little different. You're not designed to chase sales. Instead, you're designed to share your knowledge, insights, and wisdom.

Every time you do this, you create an opportunity for your audience to INVITE you to share your offers with them.

For you, every piece of content that you put out into the world needs to be optimized to bring people to your offer(s) or to join a waitlist (you'd use a waitlist for any new offers).

PS Example:
"If you feel seen, heard, and recognized by what I just shared, then I invite you to [join/check out/learn more about] xxx".

REFLECTORS: Your strategy is to FOLLOW THE LUNAR CYCLE. Because you're so open, you're being more carried along by the Universe rather than being directed like the other types.

In your SELLING activities, when it comes to presenting the opportunity, you'll want to optimize your content to link to your offer(s) or invite people to join your email list (or community, depending on your profile numbers).

PS Example:
"If you experienced the sensation of "wow, it's like xxx is in my head, how does she KNOW this?" then you will benefit from xxx".

You can craft your own soft sell PS however you wish, but I often do mine like this:

My PS Example:

P.S.: When you're ready, here are three ways I can support you right now:

- *If your next step is to build your email list, come join the List Building Collective [hyperlink]*
- *If you need daily feedback loops, peer support, and bi-monthly coaching, the Cultivate Group Program [hyperlink] is your best next step*
- *If you're more of a DIY kinda gal, then subscribing to my YouTube channel [hyperlink] where you can binge watch everything is your best option*

Ultimately, it comes down to whether you're doing an intentional promotion with your emails or you're simply sharing content.

Optimizing Your Social Profiles

When it comes to your social media profiles, you've got a lot of flexibility in how you set these up.

On your Facebook page (not profile) you'll want to ensure you've got the following set up:

- A header image that showcases your offers or the main thing you want to sell (in the description, include links)
- Several pinned/featured posts that highlight offers and freebies
- Your about section fully completed

You can see how I do that here: Hustle and Groove Facebook

On your Instagram business profile, you'll want to ensure that you've got a short bio that speaks to your ideal audience and links to an entry-level offer. You'll also likely want to have a linktree or 'link in bio' link active.

You can see how I do that here: https://www.instagram.com/lisecartwrightnz

1,266 posts   **1,779** followers   **3,194** following

Lise | Author + Biz Coach

⊖ lisecartwrightnz

Entrepreneur
☞ Stuck in the feast/famine income cycle?
📧 Follow for FREE training on marketing that works 4 u
🎥 Get Grow Your Business $5k Roadmap for $9 ↓
∅ linktr.ee/lisecartwrightnz

If you've got a YouTube channel set up, you'll definitely want to ensure you have a channel header image in place and you'll want to link to your main strategic freebie and entry-level offer.

You can see how I do that here:
https://www.youtube.com/@HustleandGroove

Lise Cartwright

@HustleandGroove · 1.13K subscribers · 259 videos

My business drastically changed when I started being intentional and strategic with the ...**more**

hustleandgroove.com/mpquizyt

Subscribe

You don't have to have these social media profiles in place. It could be your TikTok profile, your LinkedIn profile... wherever you're sharing your micro content.

The key is to ensure that your profiles reflect who you are, what you do, who you serve, and your magnetic messaging.

Notes
capture your ideas

Notes
capture your ideas

Notes

capture your ideas

NOW WHAT?

your next steps...

You Made It!
what to do next...

By now, this book should be full to the brim with your ideas, creative thoughts, answers to your burning questions, and as many scribbles as needed to get you to this point.

My intention with this book was to provide you with the space to explore how you can create content that attracts your dream clients.

We did that by first understanding our offers and audience, and then creating content from that perspective.

Then secondly, we dove headfirst into the wonderful world of Human Design and discovered additional ways that we can connect with your audience and ultimately, convert them into subscribers and buyers.

And a gentle reminder, dear reader, to **remember that it does get to be easy and fun... AND profitable!**

Once you've completed all the exercises, all that's left is to take action, create your discoverable content, and review your money-making marketing plan.

Discoverable Content fits into your NURTURE and GROW activities.

Not sure what I'm talking about? We covered this inside the Cultivate Your Cashflow book. You can check that out here: https://hustleandgroove.com/cycashflow

Don't forget to access extra templates and resources via the Resource Hub, which you'll find here: https://www.hustleandgroove.com/cyctresources

You might also be starting to feel #allthefeels... and a few new fears, challenges, and limiting beliefs are rearing their ugly heads.

It's likely that these fears, challenges, and limiting beliefs are centered around the selling of your offers. You're probably judging yourself, thinking: "Who will buy what I've created?"

You Made It!

what to do next...

Or you might be experiencing decision fatigue, overwhelm, and plain ole "I don't know what to do!" syndrome.

If that's you, then you might want to take a deep breath and simply ask yourself, *"What's my next step?"*

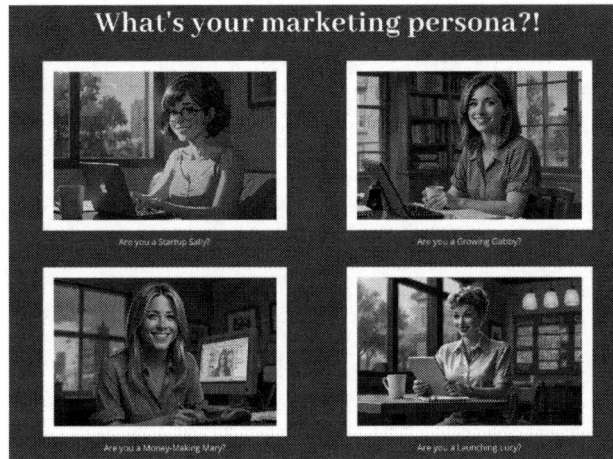

If you want to dive into your own you-nique marketing personality, take the **Marketing Persona Quiz!**

You'll find that here: https://hustleandgroove.com/mpquiz

And if you didn't get a chance to check out the main book, *Cultivate You!*, you can grab that on Amazon in both Kindle or Paperback here: https://www.hustleandgroove.com/cybbook

Good luck with it all and thanks so much for sharing your knowledge and expertise with the world.

We need people like you sharing what they know with the people who need it.

You Made It!

what to do next...

I'd also love it if you took this time to leave a review on Amazon. You can let me know what you liked and what you didn't like right there.

Or alternatively, shoot me an email with your feedback: lise@hustleandgroove.com.

And remember, you got this!

Take care,
Lise xoxo

PS: If this book resonated with you and you're ready, you might consider joining us inside the Cultivate 6-Month Group Coaching Program. It's a deep dive into the entire Cultivate Your Business book series with an online community, daily feedback, and support, as well as group coaching calls each month.

You'll find all the details here: https://www.hustleandgroove.com/cultivate

Cultivate
The 'doable' 5-Figure Monthly Income Formula
6-MONTH GROUP COACHING PROGRAM

About The Author

meet Lise Cartwright

Lise Cartwright is a bestselling author and creative business coach who is obsessed with helping others create and grow a business and life they love!

She loves curling up on a comfy couch with a good book, a hot cup of Chai Latte, and the soothing sounds of waves crashing against the white sandy beaches of the Gold Coast, Australia.

She's the founder of **www.hustleandgroove.com**, the #1 online resource for getting clear on your business model and growing an online business you are excited to work in. Her business motto is: *"if it's not easy and fun, why do it?!"*

Through her books, training videos, and coaching, she's helped thousands of people on their journey to creating an online business that's **easy**, **fun**, and **profitable**.

You can connect with Lise on the following social media platforms:

 FACEBOOK.COM/HUSTLEANDGROOVE   LINKEDIN.COM/IN/LISECARTWRIGHT

 INSTAGRAM.COM/LISECARTWRIGHTNZ

If your actions create a legacy that inspires others to dream more, learn more, do more, and become more, you're an excellent leader.

DOLLY PARTON

Notes

capture your ideas

Notes
capture your ideas

Notes

capture your ideas

Notes
capture your ideas

Printed in Great Britain
by Amazon